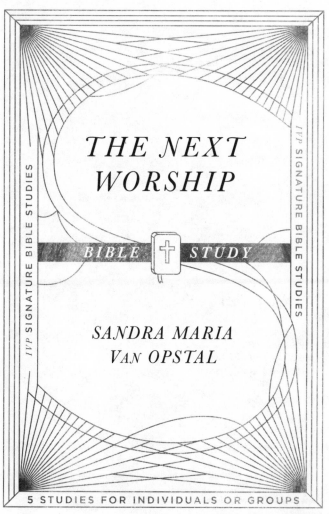

THE NEXT WORSHIP

BIBLE ✝ STUDY

SANDRA MARIA VAN OPSTAL

5 STUDIES FOR INDIVIDUALS OR GROUPS

An imprint of InterVarsity Press
Downers Grove, Illinois

InterVarsity Press
P.O. Box 1400 | Downers Grove, IL 60515-1426
ivpress.com | email@ivpress.com

InterVarsity Press® is the publishing division of InterVarsity Christian Fellowship/USA®. For more information, visit intervarsity.org.

All Scripture quotations, unless otherwise indicated, are taken from The Holy Bible, New International Version®, NIV®. Copyright © 1973, 1978, 1984, 2011 by Biblica, Inc.™ Used by permission of Zondervan. All rights reserved worldwide. www.zondervan.com. The "NIV" and "New International Version" are trademarks registered in the United States Patent and Trademark Office by Biblica, Inc.™

The publisher cannot verify the accuracy or functionality of website URLs used in this book beyond the date of publication.

Cover design and image composite: Autumn Short
Interior design: Daniel van Loon

ISBN 978-1-5140-0400-5 (print) | ISBN 978-1-5140-0401-2 (digital)

Printed in the United States of America ∞

Library of Congress Cataloging-in-Publication Data
A catalog record for this book is available from the Library of Congress.

29   28   27   26   25   24   23   22 | 13   12   11   10   9   8   7   6   5   4   3   2   1

CONTENTS

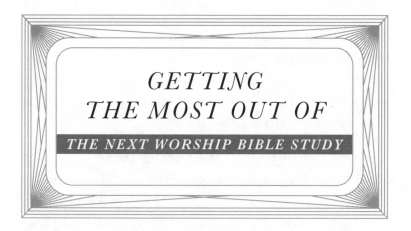

GETTING THE MOST OUT OF
THE NEXT WORSHIP BIBLE STUDY

KNOWING CHRIST is where faith begins. From there we are shaped through the essentials of discipleship: Bible study, prayer, Christian community, worship, and much more. We learn to grow in Christlike character, pursue justice, and share our faith with others. We persevere through doubts and gain wisdom for daily life. These are the topics woven into the IVP Signature Bible Studies. Working through this series will help you practice the essentials by exploring biblical truths found in classic books.

HOW IT'S PUT TOGETHER

Each session includes an opening quotation and suggested reading from the book *The Next Worship*, a session goal to help guide your study, reflection questions to stir your thoughts on the topic, the text of the Bible passage, questions for exploring the passage, response questions to help you apply what you've learned, and a closing suggestion for prayer.

The workbook format is ideal for personal study and also allows group members to prepare in advance for discussions and record discussion notes. The responses you write here can form a permanent record of your thoughts and spiritual progress.

Throughout the guide are study-note sidebars that may be useful for group leaders or individuals. These notes do not give the answers, but they do provide additional background information on certain questions and can challenge participants to think deeper or differently about the content.

WHAT KIND OF GUIDE IS THIS?

The studies are not designed to merely tell you what one person thinks. Instead, through inductive study, they will help you discover for yourself what Scripture is saying. Each study deals with a particular passage—rather than jumping around the Bible—so that you can really delve into the biblical author's meaning in that context.

The studies ask three different kinds of questions about the Bible passage:

* *Observation* questions help you to understand the content of the passage by asking about the basic facts: who, what, when, where, and how.

* *Interpretation* questions delve into the meaning of the passage.

* *Application* questions help you discover implications for growing in Christ in your own life.

These three keys unlock the treasures of the biblical writings and help you live them out.

This is a thought-provoking guide. Each question assumes a variety of answers. Many questions do not have "right" answers, particularly questions that aim at meaning or application. Instead, the questions should inspire readers to explore the passage more thoroughly.

This study guide is flexible. You can use it for individual study, but it is also great for a variety of groups—student, professional, neighborhood, or church groups. Each study takes about forty-five minutes in a group setting or thirty minutes in personal study.

SUGGESTIONS FOR INDIVIDUAL STUDY

1. This guide is based on a classic book that will enrich your spiritual life. If you have not read *The Next Worship*, you may want to read the portion recommended in the "Read" section before you begin your study. The ideas in the book will enhance your study, but the Bible text will be the focus of each session.

2. Begin each session with prayer, asking God to speak to you from his Word about this particular topic.

3. As you read the Scripture passage, reproduced for you from the New International Version, you may wish to mark phrases that seem important. Note in the margin any questions that come to your mind.

4. Close with the suggested prayer found at the end of each session. Speak to God about insights you have gained. Tell him of any desires you have for specific growth. Ask him to help you attempt to live out the principles described in that passage. You may wish to write your own prayer in this guide or a journal.

SUGGESTIONS FOR GROUP MEMBERS

Joining a Bible study group can be a great avenue to spiritual growth. Here are a few guidelines that will help you as you participate in the studies in this guide.

1. Reading the recommended portion of *The Next Worship*, before or after each session, will enhance your study and understanding of the themes in this guide.

2. These studies use methods of inductive Bible study, which focuses on a particular passage of Scripture and works on it in depth. So try to dive into the given text instead of referring to other Scripture passages.

3. Questions are designed to help a group discuss together a passage of Scripture in order to understand its content, meaning, and implications. Most people are either natural talkers or natural listeners, yet this type of study works best if all members participate more or less evenly. Try to curb any natural tendency toward either excessive talking or excessive quiet. You and the rest of the group will benefit!

4. Most questions in this guide allow for a variety of answers. If you disagree with someone else's comment, gently say so. Then explain your own point of view from the passage before you.

5. Be willing to lead a discussion, if asked. Much of the preparation for leading has already been accomplished in the writing of this guide.

6. Respect the privacy of people in your group. Many people share things within the context of a Bible study group that they do not want to be public knowledge. Assume that personal information spoken within the group setting is private, unless you are specifically told otherwise.

7. We recommend that all groups agree on a few basic guidelines. You may wish to adapt this list to your situation:

   a. Anything said in this group is considered confidential and will not be discussed outside the group unless specific permission is given to do so.

   b. We will provide time for each person present to talk if he or she feels comfortable doing so.

   c. We will talk about ourselves and our own situations, avoiding conversation about other people.

   d. We will listen attentively to each other.

   e. We will pray for each other.

8. Enjoy your study. Prepare to grow!

SUGGESTIONS FOR GROUP LEADERS

There are specific suggestions to help you in the "Leading a Small Group" section. It describes how to lead a group discussion, gives helpful tips on group dynamics, and suggests ways to deal with problems that may arise during the discussion. With such helps, someone with little or no experience can lead an effective group study. Read this section carefully, even if you are leading only one group meeting.

A FORETASTE OF THE FUTURE

WORSHIP IS NOT ONLY CONTEXTUAL but also crosscultural; it has the potential to connect the narratives of people. Revelation 7:9-12, with its depiction of a multitude "from every nation, tribe, people and language, standing before the throne and before the Lamb," gives us a picture of the kingdom community at the end of time. This passage, while familiar, should never become boring. Clearly, it's a supernatural vision.

The authority of the Lamb, Christ himself, the power of the Spirit and the majesty of God are the only things that can unite a group of people from all over the world in a common anthem! Pay attention to one day's news: civil unrest, war, ethnic cleansing, genocide, abuse, and racism plague our relationships crossculturally. I wish this were true only outside the church, but our history demands that we take a good look in the mirror and cry out to the only God who is worthy,

> Salvation belongs to our God,
> who sits on the throne,
> and to the Lamb....
> Amen!

Praise and glory
and wisdom and thanks and honor
and power and strength
be to our God for ever and ever.
Amen! (Revelation 7:10, 12)

This vision of the end can only be hoped for and lived into by recognizing how far we are from it, and the beauty and awe we will experience when we participate in it.

Our faith calls us not only to dream and hope for this day, but also to be a foretaste of the kingdom now. We today should live in the reality of the kingdom and witness what is to come. The church points to the time that is coming by modeling and living into it today. We ought not be influenced by what we see around us; we should instead live into a worship that models something distinct from the rest of the world.

Biblical community is lived out across many differences: racial, cultural, ethnic, socioeconomic, theological. In the practice of corporate worship, no matter how different we are, we share in one common narrative in which we remember we are collectively the people of God. Yes, we are many nations. Yes, those differences are significant and beautiful. Yes, they cause natural tensions. In worship, however, we recite, reflect, and remember that God has joined us together to learn from one another how to best glorify him as a corporate body.

The church has always been and will always be a multiethnic, multilingual, global community. How then do we capture people's imagination in an embodied experience in worship? How do we create space for the vision of God's people to be realized? Does everyone have to be at the same table every time? How can I learn to lead others toward this goal?

Worship is not merely about authentic personal expression but also about communal formation. As we gather in community and see God's glory, the Spirit forms us. Corporate worship is key to spiritual formation and transformation because it keeps us focused on the glory of Christ. Practicing worship gives us a space where we can agree in song, prayer, and Scripture. When Christ is exalted, proclaimed, and experienced in our worship as truly glorious, we are changed. Congregational worship is critical. It is not merely about singing songs; it's theology to music, sermon to song. As we gather together, we come as we are, but we should leave different from how we came.

Whether we come from a diverse or monocultural context, there are two primary reasons why we should engage in other cultural forms of worship. First, we experience a fuller picture of God. Not only is the variety and range of God's creativity seen and expressed in the vast artistic range of human approaches to worship (music, instruments, words, songs), but a variety of themes are also represented. Some churches would rather sing, shout, and dance about God's victory to remind us that because he is powerful we can make it through another week! Others see worship as a space where we can cry out to God in our angst because he allows us to come as we are: weak and broken. Sharing these moments with one another broadens our perspective of God; he is my Rock and Deliverer and my Comforter and Healer.

The second reason is that diverse worship leads to personal transformation. Our understanding of the church is transformed. As we worship crossculturally, we better understand our own worship as one piece of a larger community. It's like discovering we have an accent when we are around people from other parts of the country. As we experience our differences, we can more fully enjoy what it means to connect to the global church. Then we realize we are a part of a bigger family. This helps connect us to the hearts of our brothers and sisters whose lives are radically different from ours.

SESSION ONE

HEAVEN ON EARTH

REVELATION 7:9-17; 21:1-5

MURALS TELL THE STORY OF A COMMUNITY. Murals communicate the identity of the people. The images in Scripture do the same thing. They speak to the identity and the narrative of the people of God. Like murals, we are an image to people who will never read Scripture. The church is a mural that tells a story.

Multicultural worship is not entertainment. It is an act of solidarity with communities we may never meet. It is connecting our story to their story, through which the Holy Spirit brings communion. We have the opportunity to help people to see the nature of God and God's kingdom as we worship in unity but not uniformity. What does this foretaste of heaven look like?

SESSION GOAL	READ
Gain a vision for our ultimate destination as the multiethnic, multilingual, multinational family of God.	Introduction and chapter one of *The Next Worship*

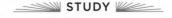

REFLECT

✳ How do cultural differences and preferences affect the way God's people worship together? Or the reasons they don't?

✳ If worship is about a collective expression, how does that reorient your understanding of the nature and purpose of a worshiping community?

STUDY

READ REVELATION 7:9-17; 21:1-5.

Consider the imagery in these passages and what it provided for the hearers. Given the persecution God's people were experiencing, the symbols were meaningful for a community that needed to hold on to hope. These images were used to encourage people who were living under an oppressive empire.

> ⁹After this I looked, and there before me was a great multitude that no one could count, from every nation, tribe, people and language, standing before the throne and before the Lamb. They were wearing white robes and were holding palm branches in their hands. ¹⁰And they cried out in a loud voice:
>
> "Salvation belongs to our God,

who sits on the throne,
and to the Lamb."

[11]All the angels were standing around the throne and around the elders and the four living creatures. They fell down on their faces before the throne and worshiped God, [12]saying:

"Amen!
Praise and glory
and wisdom and thanks and honor
and power and strength
be to our God for ever and ever.
Amen!"

[13]Then one of the elders asked me, "These in white robes—who are they, and where did they come from?"

[14]I answered, "Sir, you know."

And he said, "These are they who have come out of the great tribulation; they have washed their robes and made them white in the blood of the Lamb. [15]Therefore,

"they are before the throne of God
    and serve him day and night in his temple;
and he who sits on the throne
    will shelter them with his presence.
[16]'Never again will they hunger;
    never again will they thirst.
The sun will not beat down on them,'
    nor any scorching heat.
[17]For the Lamb at the center of the throne
    will be their shepherd;
'he will lead them to springs of living water.'
    'And God will wipe away every tear from their eyes.'"

21 Then I saw "a new heaven and a new earth," for the first heaven and the first earth had passed away, and there was no longer any sea. ²I saw the Holy City, the new Jerusalem, coming down out of heaven from God, prepared as a bride beautifully dressed for her husband. ³And I heard a loud voice from the throne saying, "Look! God's dwelling place is now among the people, and he will dwell with them. They will be his people, and God himself will be with them and be their God. ⁴"He will wipe every tear from their eyes. There will be no more death' or mourning or crying or pain, for the old order of things has passed away."

⁵He who was seated on the throne said, "I am making everything new!" Then he said, "Write this down, for these words are trustworthy and true."

1. Describe the people standing before God's throne. What are they like? What are they doing?

2. What had the worshipers experienced (vv. 14-17)?

3. What does God promise to the people in these passages?

4. What does God say about God's nature in 21:3-5?

Revelation 7:16-17 references the restoration of Israel portrayed in Isaiah 49:10. The promise in Isaiah 25:8 is also quoted in both Revelation 7 and 21. This reminds the people of the promises the former prophets had already spoken.

5. Are God's promises for an individual or for a community? What impact does this have on our reading of this passage?

6. Why is the repetition of previous promises in their history so important to God's people?

7. When communities have experienced collective and generational trauma, what can communal worship offer them? What can their theology and practice of worship offer to people who haven't had those traumatic experiences?

8. What does the promise that everything will be made new mean to people who have experienced marginalization and persecution at the hands of occupation and empire?

 RESPOND

* How can we move from differences and diversity as something to be ignored to fully embodying our diversity in our practice of worship? How can these worship moments lead to healing and restoration?

✳ What are you doing to embrace God's intended diversity, and what ideas do you have for how we should live into the future reality of the kingdom now?

✳ If at the end of all things God's people worship God together across cultures, and today cultural differences inevitably lead to tension, how might we develop individual and communal worship practices to turn our hearts away from our own preferences and comfort toward the needs of others?

> At the end of all things, our worship embodies God's creativity. God intended diversity. We have an ultimate destination as the multiethnic, multilingual, multinational family of God. This is a picture not just of diversity but of liberation, healing, restoration, and flourishing. Worship here on earth is to reflect, point to, and practice that ultimate worship experience.

 **PRAY**

Pray for our collective ability to see the nature of who God is and what God is about when we stand with one another in worship and solidarity. Pray that God will make the church a foretaste of heaven, and that people will be compelled to Christ because they see heaven on earth. Thank God that at the end of all things, God will reconcile and renew all things.

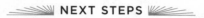

NEXT STEPS

This week, don't wait passively. Participate in the ministry of reconciliation as a form of living into God's promises and seeking healing and restoration. Make decisions about your lifestyle that point to the coming kingdom. Ask how your life might be a reflection of the power of the kingdom. Examine and name the obstacles to diverse worship, and consider creative ways to compel your community in this direction.

SESSION TWO

RECONCILED COMMUNITY

LUKE 14:15-24

GATHERING AT THE TABLE is at the center of our Christian tradition. Many scriptural images feature table fellowship. In the Old Testament, sharing a meal with someone was a sign of friendship, esteem, and social placement. In the New Testament, Jesus spent much time eating, teaching, and breaking rules at tables. Even in Jesus' last days on earth, the table was the place of his final instructions, including a command to continue to gather at the table in remembrance of him (1 Corinthians 11:23-26).

Meals provide a way for God's people to experience God as they connect with one another. Likewise in worship, as we interact in community, connecting with one another, we encounter God. This guiding image of communion at the table of Christ is central to why we participate in crosscultural worship because it invites connection with others (across differences, as Jesus modeled) and with God.

SESSION GOAL	READ
Enlarge our thoughts about God's call to intentional communion with all of God's people.	Chapters two and three of *The Next Worship*

REFLECT

✳ What are some meaningful traditions in your family that keep you connected with one another and your history?

✳ Have you ever been invited into someone else's family tradition that you enjoyed? Have you ever been invited to one that was awkward, uncomfortable, or even offensive?

STUDY

READ LUKE 14:15-24.

One of my favorite places to encounter Christ at the table is in Luke 14, where Jesus describes a master's invitation to a great banquet feast. Jesus tells this parable during a meal at the house of a prominent Pharisee (Luke 14:1). In order to truly understand the dynamics in this story, it's important not to import our own table traditions into the context.

> ¹⁵When one of those at the table with him heard this, he said to Jesus, "Blessed is the one who will eat at the feast in the kingdom of God."
>
> ¹⁶Jesus replied: "A certain man was preparing a great banquet and invited many guests. ¹⁷At the time of the

banquet he sent his servant to tell those who had been invited, 'Come, for everything is now ready.'

¹⁸"But they all alike began to make excuses. The first said, 'I have just bought a field, and I must go and see it. Please excuse me.'

¹⁹"Another said, 'I have just bought five yoke of oxen, and I'm on my way to try them out. Please excuse me.'

²⁰"Still another said, 'I just got married, so I can't come.'

²¹"The servant came back and reported this to his master. Then the owner of the house became angry and ordered his servant, 'Go out quickly into the streets and alleys of the town and bring in the poor, the crippled, the blind and the lame.'

²²"'Sir,' the servant said, 'what you ordered has been done, but there is still room.'

²³"Then the master told his servant, 'Go out to the roads and country lanes and compel them to come in, so that my house will be full. ²⁴I tell you, not one of those who were invited will get a taste of my banquet.'"

1. What is the comment that provokes Jesus' story? What does "this" refer to, and why would that have elicited this person's toast (v. 15)?

Isaiah 25:6-8 portrays God preparing a rich feast "for all peoples" with implications for the whole earth, providing a glimpse of the nature of God's kingdom. Jesus picks up this feast theme in his parable.

2. Weddings and banquets were a community experience very different from the ones we host today. Who is invited to this banquet (v. 16)?

3. How do those invited respond to the invitation? Would you buy land without seeing it or livestock without testing them out? Would you talk about your private business in front of others? What is happening here?

> When the master announced through his servant, "Come, for everything is now ready" (v. 17), he was not sending an initial invitation. In that culture, parties lasted a long time and took days to prepare, so the guests would have known in advance. The master didn't have deep freezers for his goat steaks, and when an entire village is invited, that is a lot of meat. The guests had already RSVPed to attend the banquet. Now the food has been cooked, and the guests offer excuses for not coming.

4. If the initial invites had already been received and the people rejected them late in the game, what might be the cultural significance of their rejection?

5. How does the master respond to the news of the rejections?

This master invites everyone to the table, and those who come must be willing to eat together. The invitation list reveals no favoritism. All are invited to the banquet: the social elite as well as those from the highways and byways. The tension mounts: when people from different ethnic and socioeconomic standings gather, the result is awkward dinner conversations. And let's face it, we tend to avoid parties where we expect awkwardness.

6. Why does the servant say, "what you ordered has been done" (v. 22)? What kinds of people were already invited to the party? What does this say about the master?

7. What is the hope of the master (v. 23)?

8. Why might we need to compel those on the margins to come to the feast? What might keep them from coming?

 **RESPOND**

✳ How are we tempted to reject the Master's invitation to be in community with others we'd rather not share a table with?

✳ How can we create spaces that will compel people from all walks of life who have not trusted the church would be a place of welcome?

PRAY

As you pray, thank God that those on the margins are not an afterthought but welcomed to the table. Ask God to give you compassion for those who might be slow to trust spaces in which they are underrepresented. Ask God to grant you the creativity to make a place of hospitality for people from other racial, ethnic, and socioeconomic backgrounds.

NEXT STEPS

This week consider how the practices of your church might better reflect the hospitality that God offers to those who are often subject to marginalization. Consider practical and obvious ways your congregation compels people to come and feast at the table. Take time to do the cultural values continuum in appendix A in *The Next Worship*.

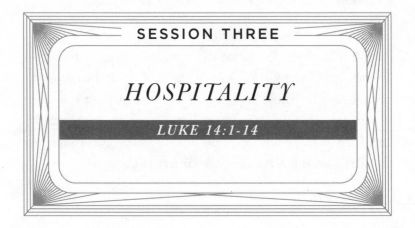

HOSPITALITY

LUKE 14:1-14

BIBLICAL COMMUNITY IS LIVED OUT across many differences: racial, cultural, ethnic, socioeconomic, theological. No matter how different we are, we share in one common narrative in which we remember we are collectively the people of God. Biblical hospitality is the embodiment of that truth. It has nothing to do with bougie church coffee shops or welcome desks. It is the particular care that we as a community give to those who are often unwelcome in our society. It is creating a practice in which those considered last will be made first. Our gatherings often marginalize those Jesus would have prioritized.

SESSION GOAL	READ
Understand the nature of biblical hospitality and consider how we communicate that welcome.	Chapter four of *The Next Worship*

✳ When you hear the word *hospitality*, what images come to mind? How did you develop those?

✳ What tangible things have you seen others do to make a person socially pushed to the margins feel embraced and honored?

───⟋⟍⟍ **STUDY** ⟋⟍⟍───

READ LUKE 14:1-14.

One Sabbath, when Jesus went to eat in the house of a prominent Pharisee, he was being carefully watched. ²There in front of him was a man suffering from abnormal swelling of his body. ³Jesus asked the Pharisees and experts in the law, "Is it lawful to heal on the Sabbath or not?" ⁴But they remained silent. So taking hold of the man, he healed him and sent him on his way.

⁵Then he asked them, "If one of you has a child or an ox that falls into a well on the Sabbath day, will you not immediately pull it out?" ⁶And they had nothing to say.

[7]When he noticed how the guests picked the places of honor at the table, he told them this parable: [8]"When someone invites you to a wedding feast, do not take the place of honor, for a person more distinguished than you may have been invited. [9]If so, the host who invited both of you will come and say to you, 'Give this person your seat.' Then, humiliated, you will have to take the least important place. [10]But when you are invited, take the lowest place, so that when your host comes, he will say to you, 'Friend, move up to a better place.' Then you will be honored in the presence of all the other guests. [11]For all those who exalt themselves will be humbled, and those who humble themselves will be exalted."

[12]Then Jesus said to his host, "When you give a luncheon or dinner, do not invite your friends, your brothers or sisters, your relatives, or your rich neighbors; if you do, they may invite you back and so you will be repaid. [13]But when you give a banquet, invite the poor, the crippled, the lame, the blind, [14]and you will be blessed. Although they cannot repay you, you will be repaid at the resurrection of the righteous."

1. Jesus chooses to see and center someone who would have been considered "unclean." What does he do once he acknowledges him?

> In the Gospels, the image of a wedding sometimes points to the final celebration in God's kingdom. See Matthew 22:1-14; 25:1-13.

2. Jesus, coming from an indirect Middle Eastern culture, spoke truth in parables to illustrate his point. What did Jesus notice the guests were doing that prompted his story in verses 8-11?

3. Who will be exalted? Who will be humiliated? What is the cause of the humiliation?

> Jesus directs this particular parable at his fellow guests who are vying for the place of honor. His instruction not only crosses boundaries but redefines them. Outsiders are in, the down are up, and the least are great. This is often called the "great reversal." It's also rooted in Luke 13:30, where Jesus says, "Indeed there are those who are last who will be first, and first who will be last."

4. This truth in verse 11 is commonly quoted when we consider
   individuals who are deliberately taking up "too much space,"
   but what about groups of people who have been in a space of
   honor? Who are some of these groups in your own context?

5. What is hard about being asked to humble oneself?

6. Then Jesus directs his attention to the host. What kinds of
   people should the host *not* invite? What kinds of people
   should the host invite? How is this a countercultural act?

7. Think about the gatherings you attend, not merely parties but anywhere people are convened. Who is there?

> In worship, we recite, reflect, and remember that God has joined us together to learn from one another how to best glorify him as a corporate body. This multiethnic worship is a place where we acknowledge, honor, and embody the diversity of the global church.

8. How might people in Jesus' day and our day regard the folks described in verse 13? Who might they blame for such people's misfortune?

9. Think about the spiritual community to which you are connected. Who is centered and celebrated as leaders and voices that are important to listen to? Do they include those who are economically and socially marginalized?

⚒ RESPOND ⚒

⁕ When people advocate for voices that are marginalized to be exalted, why do those in the place of honor often silence them? What kind of humiliation might people be feeling when someone has to ask them to step away from the place of honor when they've been occupying it for so long?

⁕ What are ways we can nurture community that consider and center those who are often not given prestige?

⚒ PRAY ⚒

As you pray, thank Jesus for warning us and inviting us to humble ourselves so that we don't have to be humiliated.

⚒ NEXT STEPS ⚒

This week think back on how you have connected with others over the last six months. Take note of how many people you've invited that resulted in more honor and prestige for you versus those who could not repay you. Make changes and model for your family and spiritual community what you think Jesus is saying in this passage.

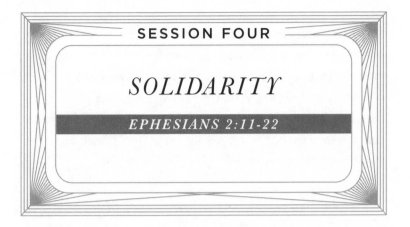

SESSION FOUR

SOLIDARITY

EPHESIANS 2:11-22

IF YOU'VE BEEN TO A WEDDING, then you've likely heard the phrase "What God has joined together, let no one separate." This is a mysterious moment we all witness in our suits, saris, guayaberas, and fancy jewelry that signifies a new reality, a reality we all know will take a lifetime to embody. It's something that is true in that moment, but that's realized as it is lived.

When I go through premarital and marriage counseling with couples, I explain that they will be "one flesh," but they will also have to work at it. They are two different people with different likes, dislikes, gifts, personalities, values, and histories. Over several sessions, we study their families of origin. We have them assess how they view finances, conflict, and sexual expectations. Real talk! It takes work to bring together the couple across all those differences.

Similarly, in the body of Christ, this mystery of oneness is true and yet often doesn't feel like it is. When we see the research on how Christians understand social issues in our world, we can see the divide. When we try to work across theological differences that are impacted by cultural preferences and racial realities, we feel the division. The oneness God invites us to, whether in marriage or in community, is a journey of self-awareness and embrace that makes us one another's fiercest allies in solidarity. This solidarity does not mean we cease to see our preferences, but it means we name our biases and then choose which ones we need to let go of or reform.

SESSION GOAL	READ
Embrace the invitation to true solidarity in Christ and learn to embody that oneness in a practical way.	Chapters five and six of *The Next Worship*

 **REFLECT**

✳ Why do you think couples should go through some form of premarital counseling to prepare for oneness? What are the benefits?

✳ The difficulties of life have shown us how divided our communities have been. Sometimes it is hard to believe in solidarity across differences. How have you seen true solidarity embodied in a tangible way?

━━▧ STUDY ▨━━

READ EPHESIANS 2:11-22.

Most of the believers in Ephesus were Gentiles. In his letter to the Ephesians, Paul contrasts their life before and after coming to Christ.

[11]Therefore, remember that formerly you who are Gentiles by birth and called "uncircumcised" by those who call themselves "the circumcision" (which is done in the body by human hands)— [12]remember that at that time you were separate from Christ, excluded from citizenship in Israel and foreigners to the covenants of the promise, without hope and without God in the world. [13]But now in Christ Jesus you who once were far away have been brought near by the blood of Christ.

[14]For he himself is our peace, who has made the two groups one and has destroyed the barrier, the dividing wall of hostility, [15]by setting aside in his flesh the law with its commands and regulations. His purpose was to create in himself one new humanity out of the two, thus making peace, [16]and in one body to reconcile both of them to God through the cross, by which he put to death their hostility. [17]He came and preached peace to you who were far away and peace to those who were near. [18]For through him we both have access to the Father by one Spirit.

[19]Consequently, you are no longer foreigners and strangers, but fellow citizens with God's people and also members of his household, [20]built on the foundation of the apostles and prophets, with Christ Jesus himself as the chief cornerstone. [21]In him the whole building is joined together and rises to become a holy temple in the Lord.

²²And in him you too are being built together to become a dwelling in which God lives by his Spirit.

> The letter to the Ephesians was sent to express to communities of faith how different peoples can live together in unity and love. It helps us understand our identity as one people (chapters 1–3) and our practice of oneness (chapters 4–6). In a world where we all struggle to get people with different ethnic, cultural, generational, and racial backgrounds to live together in peace and to build a just society, we need this word from Ephesians on solidarity.

1. How does verse 11 frame Paul's comments in verse 12? What is he inviting them to remember and why?

2. What has Jesus done, and how has he done it?

3. What has Jesus' work done for God's people (vv. 18-19)?

4. Unpack the image of the building that Paul is using to describe the family of God. What are the components of this building, and how is it built?

5. What are the common themes in the images Paul uses in this passage: citizenship, a body, a building?

6. What role does the Holy Spirit play in the unity that Paul is describing?

7. What does it mean to have unity without uniformity?

8. Why don't we often want to talk about how racial experiences and cultural values shape our spirituality in distinct ways?

9. What keeps us from standing with our brothers and sisters in pain as a way to embody solidarity? How might replacing the word *unity* with *collective flourishing* change how we live?

10. In verse 15 Paul says Jesus created oneness in humanity. Ephesians 5:31 says there is oneness in marriage: "the two will become one flesh." Compare the intentionality of realizing oneness in marriage to our intentionality of realizing oneness across cultural differences.

> Like with marriage, the theological reality is oneness, but the practical expression takes *work*! Listening, adapting, adjusting, growing, and dying to yourself. But in this work comes true oneness. We are becoming a new people, a glorious building that points to the real nature of a peacemaking God.

11. We have assurance that in the end we will be joined together. How does Paul say God's going to do it (vv. 20-22)?

RESPOND

＊ Multiethnic, multiracial, multiclass, and multigenerational
relationships are not just going to happen. They require intentionality and proximity. In what areas of your life do you need
more intentionality to help build solidarity across differences?

＊ Solidarity in worship and spiritual practices requires inter-
rogating our values. What can your community do to become
more aware of the preferences it prioritizes in formation?

PRAY

As you pray, consider these words I heard in a lecture by New
Testament scholar Dana Harris: "We need to reclaim biblical
reconciliation as the very core of the gospel. We need to reclaim

biblical diversity as the way the church images Christ. Reconciliation is the glorious work that God is doing in and through us—and diversity is the evidence of that. We will never fully image Christ until we are reconciled to the Father through the Son and bound to each other in the Spirit."

⟞⟍⟍ NEXT STEPS ⟋⟋⟍

This week take note of how you and your church have invested in preparing for oneness as a community. Consider what tools, training, or assessments you would need to practice true solidarity and make some commitments to invest time and resources into that journey.

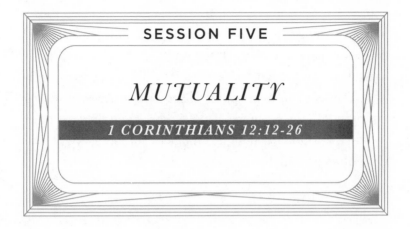

SESSION FIVE

MUTUALITY

1 CORINTHIANS 12:12-26

As we have seen so far, reconciliation in worship is expressed in hospitality and solidarity. This ultimately leads us to mutuality. Biblical reconciliation therefore calls us not only to welcome one another and stand with one another, but to depend on one another. Through congregational worship we can communicate, "We welcome you," "We are with you," and "We need you."

Over the past few years, since the beginning of the coronavirus pandemic, we have experienced collective lament and loss that many of us did not have the spiritual practices to endure. However, we do have brothers and sisters in the church who have known loving God *only* in the midst of pandemics, poverty, persecution, and pain. The songs they sing, the prayers they write, and the practices that have kept those on the social margins clinging to God are a gift to the whole. It has been life altering for me to worship God with the songs from my siblings in Egypt, the prayers from immigrant churches, and the deeply rooted theology of healing and freedom from my black sisters in the United States. This is the gift of a spirituality that says we have something to learn as we listen to one another and decenter those who have often been at the lead.

Mutuality is the last and hardest step! This last expression is what is missing in many of our diversity practices. Admitting our need for others requires that we submit ourselves to others' perspectives. God has designed the body for mutuality, but we don't often practice it.

SESSION GOAL	READ
Increase our understanding of our need for mutuality as individuals and communities.	Chapters seven and eight of *The Next Worship*

 **REFLECT**

✳ Does collaboration and input from diverse voices appeal to you? Why or why not?

✳ Think about a time when learning from others and leaning on others helped you realize a vision. Share about a time you saw communities doing this.

═══⟩⟩⟩ STUDY ⟨⟨⟨═══

READ 1 CORINTHIANS 12:12-26.

12Just as a body, though one, has many parts, but all its many parts form one body, so it is with Christ. 13For we were all baptized by one Spirit so as to form one body—whether Jews or Gentiles, slave or free—and we were all given the one Spirit to drink. 14Even so the body is not made up of one part but of many.

15Now if the foot should say, "Because I am not a hand, I do not belong to the body," it would not for that reason stop being part of the body. 16And if the ear should say, "Because I am not an eye, I do not belong to the body," it would not for that reason stop being part of the body. 17If the whole body were an eye, where would the sense of hearing be? If the whole body were an ear, where would the sense of smell be? 18But in fact God has placed the parts in the body, every one of them, just as he wanted them to be. 19If they were all one part, where would the body be? 20As it is, there are many parts, but one body.

21The eye cannot say to the hand, "I don't need you!" And the head cannot say to the feet, "I don't need you!" 22On the contrary, those parts of the body that seem to be weaker are indispensable, 23and the parts that we think are less honorable we treat with special honor. And the parts that are unpresentable are treated with special modesty, 24while our presentable parts need no special treatment. But God has put the body together, giving greater honor to the parts that lacked it, 25so that there should be no division in the body, but that its parts should have equal concern for each other. 26If one part suffers, every part suffers with it; if one part is honored, every part rejoices with it.

1. What do we share in common? What is different? (vv. 12-14)

2. What are some ways Paul explains the interdependence of the body?

3. What have some parts of the body been made to feel about themselves (vv. 15-20)?

4. What emboldens some parts of the body to view themselves as the really essential parts?

5. What are body parts not allowed to say to others? How do we communicate this message to one another?

Although the early church had diversity, the people involved did not have equal standing. When they gathered for worship it was likely the only time people of different social standings were entering through the same door. Outside the church, servants used back doors and underground passages to travel through homes and parts of town so that their presence was not detected. Jews kept kosher laws that prohibited them from touching certain foods and people or entering the homes of some people. In one of the wealthiest and most diverse cities, there was a huge disparity between the affluent and the poor. Paul had to remind them there were no second-class citizens in God's body.

This passage comes directly after Paul corrects the
Corinthians for bickering over which gifts of the Spirit
are more valuable and for how people of privilege
were abusing the table fellowship where Communion
was shared. Paul brings up these two issues together—
embracing diversity and not abusing power—because
in Greco-Roman society, people were conditioned to
believe that each person or group should perform the
hierarchically assigned roles given to them by nature.
This would prevent society from disintegrating into
chaos. Paul is using a familiar metaphor to argue there
is no such hierarchy of importance in the body of Christ.

6. How does Paul say we ought to treat the parts that are *seemingly* weak and that we *think* are less honorable? Does Paul actually say they are weaker or less honorable?

7. What are the cultural factors that cause some of us to interpret this verse merely as a call to mutuality between individuals? What meaning would this verse have if we thought of the body parts as whole communities (ethnic, racial, generational, etc.) instead of individuals?

8. What happens to the whole body when parts abuse, envy, or ignore one another? What systems create imposter syndrome for some groups of people? How is participating in these behaviors harmful?

9. How can we practice honoring parts of our community or entire communities that are marginalized?

RESPOND

* At the end of all things, Revelation 21:24-26 says, the nations will walk by the light produced by God's glory, "and the kings of the earth will bring their splendor into it. . . . The glory and honor of the nations will be brought into it." Is the church practicing this kind of mutuality in our local spaces or friendships?

✳ When we consider that only 10 percent of the global church
is in the West, what kind of changes does that invite us to
make in who we honor or position as indispensable in our
discipleship?

 **PRAY**

As you pray, name groups of people who are indispensable and
often overlooked.

 **NEXT STEPS**

Take inventory of your schedule, phone calls, podcasts, book-
shelves. Name the voices, experts, and relationships that you are
centering in your life personally. Who is being given the honor
of your ear and time? Now do this same practice for the communities in which you participate.

LEADING A SMALL GROUP

Leading a Bible discussion can be an enjoyable and rewarding experience. But it can also be intimidating—especially if you've never done it before. If this is how you feel, you're in good company.

Remember when God asked Moses to lead the Israelites out of Egypt? Moses replied, "Please send someone else" (Exodus 4:13)! But God gave Moses the help (human and divine) he needed to be a strong leader.

Leading a Bible discussion is not difficult if you follow certain guidelines. You don't need to be an expert on the Bible or a trained teacher. The suggestions listed below can help you to effectively fulfill your role as a leader—and enjoy doing it.

PREPARING FOR THE STUDY

1. As you study the passage before the group meeting, ask God to help you understand it and apply it in your own life. Unless this happens, you will not be prepared to lead others. Pray too for the various members of the group. Ask God to open your hearts to the message of his Word and motivate you to action.

2. Read the introduction to the entire guide to get an overview of the subject at hand and the issues that will be explored.

3. Be ready to respond to the "Reflect" questions with a personal story or example. The group will be only as vulnerable and open as its leader.

4. Read the chapters of the companion book that are recommended at the beginning of the session.

5. Read and reread the assigned Bible passage to familiarize yourself with it. You may want to look up the passage in a Bible so that you can see its context.

6. This study guide is based on the New International Version of the Bible. It will help you and the group if you use this translation as the basis for your study and discussion.

7. Carefully work through each question in the study. Spend time in meditation and reflection as you consider how to respond.

8. Write your thoughts and responses in the space provided in the study guide. This will help you to express your understanding of the passage clearly.

9. It might help you to have a Bible dictionary handy. Use it to look up any unfamiliar words, names, or places.

10. Take the final (application) study questions and the "Respond" portion of each study seriously. Consider what this means for your life, what changes you may need to make in your lifestyle, or what actions you can take in your church or with people you know. Remember that the group will follow your lead in responding to the studies.

LEADING THE STUDY

1. Be sure everyone in your group has a study guide and a Bible. Encourage the group to prepare beforehand for each discussion by reading the introduction to the guide and by working through the questions for that session.

2. At the beginning of your first time together, explain that these studies are meant to be discussions, not lectures. Encourage the members of the group to participate. However, do not put pressure on those who may be hesitant to speak during the first few sessions.

3. Begin the study on time. Open with prayer, asking God to help the group understand and apply the passage.

4. Have a group member read aloud the introductory paragraphs at the beginning of the discussion. This will remind the group of the topic of the study.

5. Discuss the "Reflect" questions before reading the Bible passage. These kinds of opening questions are important for several reasons. First, there is usually a stiffness that needs to be overcome before people will begin to talk openly. A good question will break the ice.

   Second, most people will have lots of different things going on in their minds (dinner, an exam, an important meeting coming up, how to get the car fixed), which have nothing to do with the study. A creative question will get their attention and draw them into the discussion.

   Third, opening questions can reveal where our thoughts or feelings need to be transformed by Scripture. That is why it is important not to read the passage before the "Reflect" questions are asked. The passage will tend to color the honest reactions people would otherwise give, because they feel they are supposed to think the way the Bible does.

6. Have a group member read aloud the Scripture passage.

7. As you ask the questions, keep in mind that they are designed to be used just as they are written. You may simply read them aloud. Or you may prefer to express them in your own words.

    There may be times when it is appropriate to deviate from the study guide. For example, a question may already have been answered. If so, move on to the next question. Or someone may raise an important question not covered in the guide. Take time to discuss it, but try to keep the group from going off on tangents.

8. Avoid offering the first answer to a study question. Repeat or rephrase questions if necessary until they are clearly understood. An eager group quickly becomes passive and silent if members think the leader will give all the *right* answers.

9. Don't be afraid of silence. People may need time to think about the question before formulating their answers.

10. Don't be content with just one answer. Ask, "What do the rest of you think?" or, "Anything else?" until several people have given answers to a question. You might point out one of the study sidebars to help spur discussion; for example, "Does the quotation on page seventeen provide any insight as you think about this question?"

11. Acknowledge all contributions. Be affirming whenever possible. Never reject an answer. If it is clearly off base, ask, "Which verse led you to that conclusion?" or, "What do the rest of you think?"

12. Don't expect every answer to be addressed to you, even though this will probably happen at first. As group members become more at ease, they will begin to truly interact with each other. This is one sign of a healthy discussion.

13. Don't be afraid of controversy. It can be stimulating! If you don't resolve an issue completely, don't be frustrated. Move on and keep it in mind for later. A subsequent study may solve the problem.

14. Try to periodically summarize what the group has said about the passage. This helps to draw together the various ideas mentioned and gives continuity to the study. But don't preach.

15. When you come to the application questions at the end of each "Study" section, be willing to keep the discussion going by describing how you have been affected by the study. It's important that we each apply the message of the passage to ourselves in a specific way.

    Depending on the makeup of your group and the length of time you've been together, you may or may not want to discuss the "Respond" section. If not, allow the group to read it and reflect on it silently. Encourage members to make specific commitments and to write them in their study guide. Ask them the following week how they did with their commitments.

16. Conclude your time together with conversational prayer. Ask for God's help in following through on the commitments you've made.

17. End the group discussion on time.

Many more suggestions and helps are found in The Big Book on Small Groups *by Jeffrey Arnold.*

THE IVP SIGNATURE COLLECTION

Since 1947 InterVarsity Press has been publishing thoughtful Christian books that serve the university, the church, and the world. In celebration of our seventy-fifth anniversary, IVP is releasing special editions of select iconic and bestselling books from throughout our history.

RELEASED IN 2019

Basic Christianity (1958)
JOHN STOTT

How to Give Away Your Faith (1966)
PAUL E. LITTLE

RELEASED IN 2020

The God Who Is There (1968)
FRANCIS A. SCHAEFFER

This Morning with God (1968)
EDITED BY CAROL ADENEY AND BILL WEIMER

The Fight (1976)
JOHN WHITE

Free at Last? (1983)
CARL F. ELLIS JR.

The Dust of Death (1973)
OS GUINNESS

The Singer (1975)
CALVIN MILLER

RELEASED IN 2021

Knowing God (1973)
J. I. PACKER

Out of the Saltshaker and Into the World
(1979) REBECCA MANLEY PIPPERT

A Long Obedience in the Same Direction
(1980) EUGENE H. PETERSON

More Than Equals (1993)
SPENCER PERKINS AND CHRIS RICE

Between Heaven and Hell (1982)
PETER KREEFT

Good News About Injustice (1999)
GARY A. HAUGEN

The Challenge of Jesus (1999)
N. T. WRIGHT

Hearing God (1999)
DALLAS WILLARD

RELEASING IN 2022

The Heart of Racial Justice (2004)
BRENDA SALTER McNEIL AND
RICK RICHARDSON

Sacred Rhythms (2006)
RUTH HALEY BARTON

Habits of the Mind (2000)
JAMES W. SIRE

True Story (2008)
JAMES CHOUNG

Scribbling in the Sand (2002)
MICHAEL CARD

The Next Worship (2015)
SANDRA MARIA VAN OPSTAL

Delighting in the Trinity (2012)
MICHAEL REEVES

Strong and Weak (2016)
ANDY CROUCH

Liturgy of the Ordinary (2016)
TISH HARRISON WARREN

IVP SIGNATURE BIBLE STUDIES

As companions to the IVP Signature Collection, IVP Signature Bible Studies feature the inductive study method, equipping individuals and groups to explore the biblical truths embedded in these books.